The American Poetry Series

Vol

D0783215

Books by Jon Anderson

Looking for Jonathan
Death & Friends
In Sepia
Counting the Days
Cypresses

THE MILKY WAY

POEMS 1967-1982

JON ANDERSON

THE MILKY WAY

POEMS 1967-1982

The Ecco Press · New York

First published by The Ecco Press in 1983
18 West 30th Street, New York, N.Y. 10001
Published simultaneously in Canada by
George J. McLeod, Limited, Toronto, Canada
Printed in the United States of America
The Ecco Press logo by Ahmed Yacoubi
Designed by Cynthia Krupat
First Edition
Library of Congress Cataloging in Publication Data
Anderson, Jon / The Milky Way
(American poetry series, vol. 25)
I. Title   II. Series
PS3551.N37M5   1983   811'.54   82-11491
ISBN 0-88001-006-1

for Barbara & Bodi

Acknowledgments

Grateful acknowledgment is made to The University of Pittsburgh Press for permission to reprint poems from *Looking for Jonathan, Death & Friends,* and *In Sepia.*
I would like to express my gratitude to Scott Walker, whose Graywolf Press published many of the new poems in a volume entitled *Cypresses.*
Some of the poems in *American Landscape with Clouds & a Zoo* first appeared in the following magazines: *Antaeus, Antioch Review, Crazy Horse, Field, Iowa Review, Sonora Review, Porch.*
I would like to thank the John Simon Guggenheim Foundation, the National Endowment for the Arts, and the Centrum Foundation of the Washington State Commission on the Arts for grants which made completion of *The Milky Way* possible.
Lastly, my thanks to Bruce Cohen, David Rivard, George Shelton, and Julie Willson, whose suggestions aided me greatly in the choosing and arranging of these poems.

Contents

AMERICAN LANDSCAPE

WITH CLOUDS & A ZOO

[NEW POEMS]

LOOKING FOR JONATHAN

[1968]

DEATH & FRIENDS

[1970]

I

IN SEPIA

[1 9 7 4]

I

AMERICAN LANDSCAPE

WITH CLOUDS &

A ZOO

[NEW POEMS]

Let nothing be changed and all be different.

ROBERT BRESSON
Notes on Cinematography

I

A PROLOGUE

FOR FRANCIS JAMMES

Please examine this book. It was invented
By a man named Francis Jammes of Orthez.

You see he has sewn the words together
As you & I might garden: with care for color,

A certain ardor, a certain order, then
We're off to play quoits with a friend.

Some measure of the casual depends on care:
To live at home & not remain a child.

Jammes lived with his mother most of his years;
Alas, a life of suffering! How else to live?

Though finally he married a girl who admired his words
& probably read her some of his, then, new work:

This about suffering. This about God's world,
Where the child thinks the measure of things

Is weighed on the grocer's great tin scale.
Are there numbers that don't divide us then?

There are a number of poems he hadn't the time to write.
Please examine these. Tell him what you think.

AMERICAN LANDSCAPE
WITH CLOUDS & A ZOO

You can be walking along the beach
Of a quaint Northwestern coastal town
On the one hand the great Pacific Ocean
Held placid, restless, in the Sound
When it comes over: like those immense,
Woollen-gray clouds, layer upon layer,
That pour from their Pacific composure
Suddenly troubled, moving, troubling,
Roaring easterly overhead for the inland.
America is in trouble & you're too
Fucked-up to even understand, buy it.
Is America fucked-up because it understands
Itself only too well as you do you?
Every time your girlfriend chucks you
A lusciously coy smile, you're beside
Yourself like a sailboat & every time
You think happiness is just like this,
Forever, you're fooled, like a kid.

America, I'm glad I'm hardly you,
I've got myself to think about.
In my zone is a fairly large zoo,
Plenty of room to walk around; shade,
& the shade that is increasingly, bitterly,
Called shadow. Of animals there are but 2,
Arranged in unpredictable cadence & sequence.
One is the renowned leopard of the snow:
Lazy, humorous, speckled pepper a bit—
Like the wren that flies from shadow to cage
To shade to shadow. When I mistakenly
Awaken at night, I dread both the darkness

& the inevitable increasingly querulous
Birdsong of the inevitable increasingly
Wide stun of light. Everything
Is too brief, eternal, stable, unpredictable.
Everything always says, I'm all there is
Forever, chum, just see it my way, & I do.

SONNET

THINKING OF DEATH

1955

Boughs over the courthouse pattern. By afternoon
Chill air, sun a slightly aslant pale wafer, paper sky.
The birds' plumage seemed darker every day.
Living in Breughel's palette of red-browns, reds,
Walked sometimes the ½ mile from high school home
In a literal blizzard of leaves & birds asway
Heady with the edge of a new knowledge
Coming. My way. It had a glide, a leap,
A pause in the local atmosphere, snap
Jump-shot, a quick look out over everything
Nearby; it had the ivory intellectual look
Of the bald moon rising: a wonder, a stone
Afloat, a stepping stone, so step
Upon it, think, think upon it. Smart boy.

CAMOUFLAGE

Then it was autumn & the leaves fell down,
    Full of the odors of tobacco
& coffee; when the uncles burped & smoked,
    Repeated their little histories
Because weren't they after all still children?
    & you hid your secret body in the room,
Behind the drapes, down-flowing as a coming rain,
    Wrapping yourself in such robes
Of velvet-&-lilac-patterns of crimson—
    An India from which to listen:

And began to be not so taken with life's
    Events: a meal, a coming storm.
But *nuance*—yes, that was the tangible thing
    A child's body could take in—
A connection from this day to that one.
    Like the seasons: their terrible
Seemingly effortless labor to simply *become*.
    So you turned briefly to the storm,
Where in the distance some men in a camouflage
    Of coats were just beginning to run.

LIVES OF THE SAINTS

PART I

This is the rain on Mozart's grave,
Shearing to glissandi.
Where do you little lie, exhausted, whole,
& wholly done?
Sweet Amadeus,
When I sip my bourbon,
Weaving myself toward pure abstraction—
The recollection
Of emotion without the tired events—
I'd trade my part in this to bear your song:
Even the most,
Last, broken, Wolfgang, human moan.
You are so friendly, & your pillow is a stone.

This is Mozart:
A curtain of rain,
The turning heads of certain women,
The sweetness of bourbon,
Sweetness of music
The poor politeness of oblivion.

•

"Dear Sir
I am in a Madhouse & quite
Forget your Name or who you are
You must excuse me
For I have nothing to communicate
Or tell & why
I am shut up I don't know
I have nothing to say so must conclude

Yours respectfully
John Clare"

Was this his letter into the earth?
Was it wholly composed
Of solitude?
It was wholly composed.
Did he bear extravagant pain,
Whose poems, of such light fragrance
As to be
(Dear Sir, forgive me) small?
You are minor, Sir, & would not offend.
I am, respectfully
Yours.

.

Under the gathering, luminous clouds
He walked his grounds, thought:
Another reigns:
I must not, Tolstoi, be myself!
& fled from home.
We have the early flickering films,
The mourning strangers, waving.
All day
He lay at Astapovo Station,
Over & over: "I do not understand
What it is I have to do!"

"Yes, one good deed,
A cup of water, given . . ."
Prevailed: his gentleness, his pride,
Who would not bow
(The light: a small tin lamp w / o a shade)
To read himself:
"I have no passport,
I am a servant of God."

．

The age demanded acquiescence.
Stalin's cock, a stone.
The heart
Of Mandelstam, in exile, pumps & dries.
The bells of Petrograd,
The bells of Leningrad,
Limed with ice,
Are hollow;
Silence stalks the frozen snow.

We threw our matches
Three times in our Yankee vodka,
Hoping for a conflagration—
Anger!
For Mandelstam, for Mayakovsky,
Anna Akhmatova!
For timid Mandelstam, three times a fool,
Accused & blessed:
Poet!   Russian!   Jew!

．

I am Chopin,
I enclose a little time,
I bow & play:
The sea, the chandelier, this room, the sky,
The cliffs at Sourash,
Even the whole of Europe,
Blown black, spin—
The music speeds . . . retreats . . .
& I am Robert Schumann,
Mad & done,
Yet must, a little time, go on.

Now
At the hour we lately lie awake,
Give us that surety
On which our fragile art depends.
I am Robert Schumann,
Bewildered, woken
By a strange sonata in a foreign bed.
Give me a little time—
Eternity—
& I will mend.

MEMORY: A VISION

At twilight you do what you can
Which is almost nothing.
For the coming night
Is childlike in its evocation:
The knowledge your life wears,
An overcoat over a wind.

Often in this dull radiance you take for home
You go out walking:
In the light rain before a storm
When the wind
Freshens itself along
The weed tops, the light
Races & shifts its massive pattern
& the wood groans, waking.

And once you turned,
In the flash of distant lightning
You saw the horses,
Barn & house, the forest, frozen
As if in anguish,
A line of burnt-out silhouettes
Swept beneath a lowering hand.

Aeneis, having borne his father
Out of Troy
By dark, upon his shoulders, turned,
Cast himself back along the ruined streets
Crying, all night, Creussa's name.
Because he could not
Save everything, or nothing,
He came to cast himself, in longing,
Upon the wine-dark sea.

If memory is remorse,
The terrible lightning before a storm,
Wherein the past
Lies lit, specific,
In all its tragic stasis. . .
Still, to live without it is to live alone.

In Dresden
When the buildings blazed to heaven
& the walls came tumbling down
Slow-motion,
Rising amid the sunlit dust & ash. . .
Those inner rooms, the brilliant
Artifacts of life abandoned.

Maybe the past is neither found nor lost,
But misconceived;
The future dies of fear.
If memory is remorse,
The present its rapt borderline,
You must descend a gradual ladder of grass
Into the childish earth
Now, before the wind's fist,
The storm,
The earth's darkening.

THE MILKY WAY

When I was a boy, the Milky Way
 Floated just over the City
Of Boston, so I was lucky to live
 In that place, that
House where my father lathered
 His face & like the moon
Went out, came back, walking
 Winter nights beneath
The Milky Way. Few thoughts,
 Few fears, a way of
Sleeping through the night.

 When my son lay sewn
To the sheets, adrift in his
 Diabetic coma among
The blown, seductive stars,
 I could not think of
Anything to say, for he was
 Not anywhere nearby.
He said *Papa* & came back.
 Tonight, in his play
He captains a sleek starship
 Toward the Milky Way.

When I was a boy, the City of
 Boston lay miles away
Within our sight. Evenings we
 Set our chairs upon
The lawn & talked. Few thoughts,
 A way of watching until
Dark. Then as our small wickers
 Floated through the night

I wished I might be taken away
  To live forever in that
Distant city made wholly of light.

II

THE FACE OF DÜRER

Is, perhaps, the face of Christ,
Had he a moment alone in the jail
At the City of Jerusalem, just
Before his deliverance to another
Intelligent enough to both ritualize
The judgment & absolve himself. Thus,
Perhaps the honest face of Pilate, also.
Men like this recognize each other,
Are aware of the burden of another's
Seriousness which justifies their own.

I, Albrecht Dürer the Northerner,
Have painted my own portrait here
In the proper colors at the age of 28.
Outside, it is 1500: the world is crazed
With its own ending, is allowed
No believable consolation. Sometimes
At midday only the rumble of carts
May be heard. All he is doing
Is bearing witness to himself, though
He will be the 1st and last of us to do so.

No revelation, none at all.
Unless his genius is itself
The progress of revelation.
The figure emerges from its black
Background. The hand's singular
Gesture, the face it helps identify,
Identify the future: there will be no
Plague, no further wars or oppressors.
We shall stand like this a long time,
As before a mirror, as before one another.

for Gail Orlen

WITNESS

Now "you," if you are still yourself,
Remembered, remembering,
An homage to the passage of days floating—
Pale jets of water on a millionaire's lawn
You pass some moments
In a car—

"You" must extend yourself
As, perhaps, a hand might apply light pigment
On a stucco wall, meaning
To fill in, not contour, but color,
A tint which will reveal the texture

Of an otherwise sallow face:
It is the face of Dürer! Wrapped, below, in furs
A single seemingly arthritic hand
At once clutches to him & makes the gesture
We must not mistake the meaning of:

He *is* himself,
As we are not, having come to this
Self-witnessing through so many days
Of informed, almost public, conjecture;
So, if you are not yourself, neither

Are you any other. That passing car,
Funereal in its steady pace,
Can only be ominous, so you pull the drapes
Only to lean back, weary, in your chair:
Another day, & all that money can buy—

The immense house glutted with memorabilia—
The lawn now darkening,

The strict spokes of a few trees
Will not buy back, though
It is night & already there are stars.

HOMAGE TO
ROBERT BRESSON

Spaces await their people.
An alabaster row of public urinals.
 An empty theater. A table,
Chairs, on oak door, heavily grained,
 Brass knob turning & who
Shall enter, already lost forever

 In their lives? Now
Will a soul reveal its human face,
 Secret luminous flesh,
& because the soul is speechless
 There will be little talk,
Better revealed in this single plate

 Set like a day-moon or
Lidless eye before its chair.
 Who sits shall eat, because
It is important to stay alive, to
 Bear the soul's countenance
Down into the streets, their traffic,

 Its endless movement. Here
A young priest, shaken, prays to give
 False solace to the dying;
A girl, too young, casually prepares
 To drown. Why are these
Forsaken, too long in anguish?

 Why does the tree bear leaves,
The water bear downward into the earth?
 This is the law, the rest

A commentary. She takes off her clothes,
  Folding them. He enters
A room. Though nothing can be done,

  They are not resigned.

LIVES OF THE SAINTS

PART II

A massive disorder clarified,
The land bordered
By a gray sea, smoking sky;
The masses:
Herded, inconsolable, confused.
No sword, coinage,
Two lovers with a lute,
Courtly grace, placation, will survive.
The Triumph of Death
Pieter Brueghel,
c. 1565.

And at the center
Death,
The Master,
Astride a long gaunt horse
Sweeps, adamant, his scythe,
Who from his Legion
Is in no further manner individuated.

•

In Paris, in 193–, a gaunt man
& an overcoat were leaning on a stone.
Soon gone.
Much later, was revered & read
By we, who suffer what? the world? ourselves?
For which no cause
Has yet been found.
At the end of a long hunger something
Personal hangs:
César Vallejo is dead.

Who had no Guggenheim,
No Pulitzer, or NBA, or help;
Who had no references.
But some of us
Would crawl some miles
To bring him wine & bread,
Some fruit, some candy, cars, a house,
Some care,
Our hopelessness, our dread.

·

What they suffered those seven years
At Charlestown death-house
No human tongue
Can say. Yet said:
"If it had not been for these thing,
I might have live out my life
Talking at street corners
To scorning men . . .
Belongs to us . . .
The taking of our lives."

Inasmuch as you, Bartolomeo Vanzetti,
Have clearly proven
Your existence,
We, Massachusetts, sentence you to hell.
(In the grave
The accusations, reasonable or false,
Are insubstantial
& they rot—
Yet if not for such as these
How should we accuse, atone ourselves?)

·

This is the face of a man,
His countenance,

His fact.
This, a woman's, pensive, reading.
These human, many
Heavy eyelids,
Brows, in sorrow, meditation—
These are the serial of experience restrained.
Chiaroscuro.
The light from within.

Rembrandt, we have
You more than forty years
In self-portraiture:
A public diary, confession, pose.
Also these many others:
Nameless as our many selves,
Intimate, as reminiscent
Of a look we once withheld, another given.

•

"I cannot be taken up
In this world,
I am as much at home
With the Dead as the Unborn—
Nearer the heart
Of creation than is safe, yet
Still too far."
Journals.
Berne: 1940: inscribed on Paul Klee's stone.

Tod und Feuer
(*Death & Fire 1940*)
This small, somber oil
In shades of brown,
Like most of the last, a mask:
Who revealed so much of us we cannot find,
Made passage in disguise.

The figure's grin:
A rictus?
A bemused, or enigmatic, smile?

LOVE

If he had been before alone, now he was lost; he carried himself in that manner by which young men seem mourners enclosed in cassocks of personal grief. We, who had not dared wish more than a nod of the thin, handsome face, were now downcast at his approach—which was seldom.

> *Sylvia has been strolling her garden*
> *All morning, down past the cypresses*
> *To the gardener's little yellow tool house,*
> *Then back to where the coffee stands,*
> *A wicker table, two fraying chairs.*
> *She is not in love. She has nothing to do.*

When his parents came, the one a wren, the other a thrush, to pick up his few belongings, he had not been seen in two weeks, & then ceaselessly walking between the Cathedral & Zinc Bar. Though he watched them from a door: one nervous, the other a small brown songbird in a speckled dress.

TO ENTERTAIN ROSTAND

—author of Cyrano, he was struck & killed by a block
of wood discarded from a nearby balcony

Two guys are strolling down the avenue, pleased with themselves. One is thinking about the other's wife, the other about his. This turns out to be a passing fancy, for a taxicab about to slam a DeSoto now takes their attention. Abruptly.

Two guys, two (sort of) identical thoughts in the same order.

Seeing a granite cornice, festooned lightly with the harbingers of spring, is, at this moment, suspended about three-feet, mid-air, above the head of one . . .

Does this not entertain?

THE TIME MACHINE

In *Pandora's Box,* a silence of almost
   Two hours, conceived largely
By its meticulous director, G. W. Pabst,
   There is a moment (perhaps
Of thirty frames, a second or two) when
   A woman who is on trial—
Because she both has & has not
   Murdered the lover she
Had married earlier that same day,
   But that is another story—

Sits. Her name is Louise Brooks;
   She is still alive & was
Then one of the most beautiful
   Naturally animated images
Which has been memorized by the
   Motion of film. She appears,
As those few we sometimes notice,
   Usually in passing, who
Wholly belong to this particular planet
   We've set afloat. I think

Of them as animals. They are beyond
   My envy, they are almost
Beyond my comprehension, so I think
   Wherever she lives, an
Elderly woman, she is doing well.
   Two men have just spoken
Passionately—of her, almost *to* her—
   One raised his hand, pointed,
Then swept her from the earth, for
   She is its abomination,

Is the world hurling its massive will,
    Again & again, around its
Fiery sun and it will have its way.
    To the other man I think
She is like the animals I described:
    He sees her in passing.
Both are accurate. The film is proof.
    And the film's silence
Is now accurate, for she has risen
    For judgment, hears perhaps

The projector's whirring revolutions
    Only, & they are distant.
When the word is spoken, we *see* it,
    It casts her down so
Swiftly, not even a moment. Then,
    For a moment, the veil she
Has earlier let down upon her face—
    And you will not ever,
Having seen it, forget her face—
    The veil, though dark, so

Delicate it *seems* transparent,
    Turns lightly to one
Side, as if an afterthought of
    Her body's downward
Momentum—its edge, momentarily
    Taking the graceful shape
Of that loop by which we signify
    Infinity. Though, of
Course, it is meaningless, only
    The film's perfect memory.

for Patrick Hoctel

III

WINTER LIGHT

1

The curious, compelling way in which the light
  Was sourceless, not so much dimming
As withdrawing: from the white houses, their
  Minute flakes of white paint in that
Light giving them the rough appearance of reality:
  Something to be stored & remembered.

No, I couldn't have seen that, walking home
  From school in rubber boots. I had
A pencil box: a neat little representation
  Of the great official world. My
Principal was Mr. Sukeforth, brother of
  The man who signed Jackie Robinson

In another life just after the War. When
  I asked him, he just beamed! so now
I remember that people are a source of light,
  And now, that all that litter of people
& things was what I loved but taught myself
  Too well & for no reason to forget.

2

Is it possible that we will remember awhile,
  That the process of death will be
A dimming, a lying will-less, emotionless,
  Far beneath whatever is going on,
While certain unchosen images gradually
  Slow to shadow in the mind? If

We dream, then we must take something serious
   From the world, but *what* we dream
Is so often a curiosity we can't quite place.
   I was thinking about two friends:
Strangers to each other & equally loved,
   In my dream they met. Now

I would like to lie down under a great New
   England oak, to practice breathing
Awhile. I believe it would signify some things
   Important, some things that have
No serious advantage in the world, but are
   Toys: sleeping, falling in love . . .

TUCSON: A POEM ABOUT WOOD

Jesus, the wind blew, hard, for the 1st time in ten hot
    days tonight.
We opened windows & doors. I tried to read.
I wished my son, 3, was awake, so we could have per-
    fectly talked.

I don't start to talk or read the way I start to write.

My best friend, who I'm gladdened to live alongside,
& three young men are enclosing his porch next door:
Four upright beams, a top, then a window or space for
    it—

Wood. I would like to have helped that fragile, gathering
    shape,
Especially to have hammered the frame that will hold
    glass,
But then I wouldn't have seen it, or my friends, working.

I write for something to do, so I do it;
It tells me how I am or it sometimes lies.
I hate it, I do it for pleasure, I'm not even part of it,

Though it's something like a frame & I see through it.
I see you carrying on.
I see the part of your labor that must be your pleasure.

for Steve Orlen

39

FALLING IN LOVE

VIVIAN

1

The bird on the wire was an accident.
October, a kingdom. Then rains came

&, attendant, your short, thick hair,

A recent harvest, like oranges, pungent.

Singular the zoo, its late collection of wonders:
Discreet plumage, rounded shoulders:

& how do you like my valentine derrière?
I have always enjoyed the movies.

Dodging traffic, hand-in-hand,
Like woolly Parisian lapdogs or lovers,

Gaze: *imbecile lunaire.*

2

Abrupt & charming mover,
Look how the swallows dart, loop, twine

& intertwine, a passing
Glance in the broad blue sky.

Hilarious sparrows. Cricket & music & faucet:
Our nightly counterpoint.

Vivaldi's viola, Fauré's flute,
A laughing fit,

Warm glove of your vagina,
I, the aggressor—pointed & slightly confused—

Abrupt & charming mover.

3

Yet even as you now beside me lie breathing,
How well I do not remember what brought us here,

It is not given: the bird on the wire,
Late leafy breath of October—

Not with enough precision.
The dusky gourdlike eggplant

We will batter & fry come morning
Adorns the kitchen table,

A little shade of vegetable contemplation.
I think it is lonely.

I think it would like you to awaken.

A GLOBE OF SNOW

Reading your poems, I
Remember when thought
Was the same as feeling.
When anxiety was slightly
Estranged curiosity.
I remember a globe of snow
My father turned, idly,
Beneath the parlor lamp's
Rose shade: static &
"Moonlight Serenade" drift
Out of the arched, gigantic
Philco, our grained & polished
Floor-sized radio. Love
To a child was a globe
Of moonlight, mysterious,
Waxing bright then dim.
Continuous, though.
I remember to see the great
Globe & the little, like
Ivory, almost pure.
One night in your living
Room in Colorado, we
Got high & stomped the beat
To Waylon Jennings' version
Of "Lucille." I liked you
Then, mostly a stranger,
The way I like Tu Fu,
A gentleman of tact
Whose poems nevertheless
Assume a mutual understanding:
Love of the passing, ghostly

World we live alongside &
It is almost mostly true.

for William Matthews

In a yard near Brooks' Pond
In a lattice of turning shadows
   Cast below apple branches
My grandfather stands. I am
   Almost three, witless,
Yet will remember his attitude,
   Its ease. Also sunlight,
The delicate ponderous movement
   Of the tree above him,
Remember because he then stood
   At the exact center
Of everything that matters.

   Amateur painter; amateur
Photographer. For thirty years
   I have not seen those
Tiny gray-white sunsets which
   Were set to color by
His hand. A man of patience,
   So those photographs,
Lavish minute windows, flicker
   Their little intensities
Past me yet, as if particular
   Landscapes seen speeding
From my Lionel electric train.

   Everything that matters:
Patience, the green-gold light
   Off apple branches. Now
He laughs, bows lightly to lift
   & clip a bit of ash-
Blond hair from behind my ear.
   This he will tape to

A wooden match & make a faerie
    Brush. That the clouds
May have color, the tree bear
    Its intricate lattice
Of sunlight, the child remember.

for Jack Ladd

HUNTERS IN THE SNOW

Once I lived in a big white house
Or yellow . . . maybe the sun did that.

Amid trees: cedar & the birch
Whose skin is like a white, slick parchment,

Black where torn. A gentleman,
Though awkwardly knobbed & slender.

·

In Brueghel's *Hunters in the Snow*
The trees,

Which might be cedar, recede downhill,
An indicated line

The three returning figures, tired,
Will cross then follow.

This is a line of thought,
Pieter Brueghel's, to guide them down & home.

·

I lived in Massachusetts.
Each winter was a calendar of snow,

Pages so white, so
Slowly turned I couldn't then.

Down the small New England hills
The *Flexible Flyers* sped,

A sled as good as its name;
By dusk

Many faint traceries criss-crossed,
Random & elaborate. . .

.

Someone once loaned me a book of snow.
Photographed on black,

Intricate cyrstals,
Line by line,

I read them for awhile then slept.
When I woke at dusk

Before my house
Appeared many small figures

All swathed in bunched & knotted colors,
Trudging home.

.

What a blossom
Of thought, what a snowflake

To melt on the long dark arm of your coat:
To *be* a child & *not!*

Once I lived in a big white house
In a world of snow

Where on the kitchen wall
Suspended forever

Above the great DECEMBER
Was Pieter Brueghel's *Hunters in the Snow*.

47

THE CYPRESSES

Of the leaning cypresses,
Franconati says, *These*
Feathers constitute an evidence
Or inclination of God's breath.
Seeing them from my study window
They are a gesture I begin
To understand: as the raised
Open hand, in farewell,
Salutes a depth of feeling.
Now the great ocean of wind moves,
Again the cypresses lean

& whatever their meaning,
It is a dignification, a rational
Grace, because the weight
Of even the topmost parts moves
In its own time. The wind
Is an ocean. A great armada
Of ships, pennants awash, rushes
To the horizon. They are on
An important errand, but will return
Bearing men haggard with war &
Having lived too long with the quick,
Bright meaningless striking of oars.

So this story, or poetry, first told
Among savages who were kings
In a land of cypresses by a man
Who was blind, unwinds its
Thousands of cadences: the dead are
Risen & the imagined countenanced.
When the cypresses lean again
I notice their light, slow

Tracings upon a sky full of clouds
Assuming familiar shapes;
In time, upon all the possible
Faces of all possible things.

LOOKING FOR

JONATHAN

(1968)

Jim would have liked their ashes to be mingled;

Catherine, to have hers scattered to the winds.

But it was not permitted.

JULES AND JIM

NOT LOVES, I THINK, BUT
SHAPES THEY LEAVE BEHIND

You remember how it was:

She was always alone.
   (Her one small room. Remember?)
And she was always in.
And she was always kind to us,
who cared for her.

Still, she would sometimes cry.
You remember, how she cried their names:
that high, small sound
   (you said like birds).
Your father and I
would carry her through all the rooms.
And she would count the rooms

and listen (I wondered what she heard)
and take their objects up.
Vases, figurines. Her hands
turning over each dear shape
   (you wondered what she found)
and how her hands
would simulate each shape
after she had placed it down.

BENEDICITE

Sir, here on my table
is a miracle:
two cups, white
upon the white folds
of the cloth, and milk,
and breakfast rolls.
These we had planned,
and have survived
our mortal sleep.
Behind you the window
opens outward;
light sits upon
your shoulder
like the Morning Angel:
round and vigilant.
Though we are private,
temporary things
we will, this once,
take milk and bread
and be companions of
a common table.
Then if our animal hearts
desire it, we may,
like clear water
over stones, go outward
into a meeting with
the formal shapes of day.

VOYAGE

So, at last, we *will* cross.
Our season presupposes continents, lands
of desire. We toss
like unloved baggage where we stand,

and slowly the land gives over.
Good-bye; good-bye.
The water
rises and hisses; distance simplifies

trees, houses. The small land speeds.
And we escape.

Here is your flying sea,
proportionless, your seascape

hung with birds, your frail launch
lightly bearing us in mist.
Everything's touch;
immediate. We had this

journeying at heart; yes, days
of it, weeks, buoyant, propelled.
The casual waves
blur like lines cast back. We have ourselves

out here; what else?
Birds fail. The sea shines
daily, is calm and—who can tell?—
bottomless. There will be time.

And here I awakened into fear—
a destination, as your own;

an inlet, where
the waters shine

in welcome, where the journey
cries out: *Here,* where stones, enormous,
burrow in the sea.
The shoreline grows

specific, black and real.
Here is your consummate island;
mine. The sea is still.
The launch glides inland.

We stand in this full calm,
a journey's
end. Friend, be kind,
foreshadow me.

for Joseph de Roche

PARIS

Lying beside you
I was hurt

by the lightness
of your breath.

Will you die?
I think of Paris, where

it is beginning
to be morning: Boys

ride bicycles
over the wet streets,

a slow trail warms, evaporates . . .
I will be homeless again.

THE SUMMER DEATHS

The year we
came upon
the fox's skull
I think that
I was still
in love with
life. Then, that
peculiar
fragrance of
the calm bone
thrilled, until
the very
dolphins of
the airy
summer light
dipped, nuzzled
us with love
of . . . what? Death?
We survived.
Dark angels,
like the leaves'
soft shadows,
rubbed our hearts.
But no one died.

What was your name? You
were my first love at
the summer lake. That
year the cold blue

waters brought me up,
lean and wet, into
your first, hard kiss. Oh,
you were perverse! But

I buried my face
in your crisp black hair,
tongued the dampness there,
and your wild heart raced.

And you were better
than a boy! You came
apart. And the same
feminine rage tore

in me when we lay
down. Ah, my sweet
bitch, you ripped my heart,
but I took yours away.

3

Christ, I was twelve
when I gave up my love
to you & burned in your streaming
wounds. I was the skinniest
kid in camp; I dreamed;
I faithfully wet
my bed. Only your wilderness,
berries and nuts, red
bushes gone to flame,
kept me apart
from each ordered day.
For one whole month
(August) I imagined your delicate
hands, your red mouth

pushing at my flesh. But,
in truth, it was your marvelous,
intricate pain that was temptation.
My dear Christ,
how often you came at night
redeeming some of us
(who *knew*)
from the counselor's planned salvations.
How I loved you.
Out of the dark your pale, intense
teen-ager's face
swayed behind our tent.
O, I'm here, come out, I'm here . . .
Whatever we learned
we learned through our disgrace
at being twelve, and not yet
willing to tear at
our loins, or to burn
in our private, downy hair
for love of you.

4
———

DiMaggio, Pesky,
Williams, Stephens, Doerr,
Goodman, Zarilla,
Tebbetts, Parnell or

Kinder: men, you lost
it all by just one game.
One! Damn! One! Every
year it was the same

bad story. Fly balls
to the fence. And sweat.

———

The long slide into
third. The easy out.

And the seasons slipped,
like us, from the park.
O the pale snow soars,
soars in the outfield dark.

5
_____

In a far recess of summer
monks are playing soccer.

Between the damp leaves
we can barely hear their calls

coming, or the soft leather
punt of the ball. But I'd rather

not remember. Their distant
passionless cries were hesitant

in the trees. I kissed
the book I read. I caressed

the smooth defenseless underside of
your arm. Another love,

I have put you away
in the safety of the way

those far monks joyously cried,
and you are foreign at my side.

THE ANGEL OF DEPARTURES

Continents watch through windows.
The lovers sleep, the trees
lean into their shadows.
Coming between stars,
the eye of the angel rises.
He is boyish, shy.

Illusionless, the earth
reverses beneath his stare;
the seas shine—but briefly.
Though even the deepest
waters have exchanged,
it is in a decent dream.

Now the lovers awaken
into a clear morning.
They appear to be touching.
We watch them walk
beneath the changed, black
boughs, the sons you will
never sustain, the poems
I will not begin again.

THE BLUE ANIMALS

When I awoke this morning
they were there, just as blue
as the morning, as calm
as the long green lawn

they grazed upon, turning
their delicate heads. You
would have said: No harm
shall befall us. But you were gone.

So these two opened my morning
gracefully wide and blue
as the morning sky. Their calm
mouths moved over the lawn,

and as I was turning
to call out again for you,
I saw there was no harm
at all, though you were gone.

IT IS MORNING; THE ANIMALS

It is morning; the animals
have come back, awake, amid seasons
of themselves. Walking under the arced boughs
and the moon, they have remembered
the dream they are living now,
and yesterday, and when the water
became more subtle, into marsh, and then land.
They come with only a little caution,
the lizard extending his tongue
into the sunlight, zebras
becoming blond, the raccoon
reaching into newness, toward death.
One pale lion turns on its back,
dreaming in the grass which is bloodied
and bright. In his dream he says: *My friend.*

And it is true. Each animal
stands in its green contemplative room,
even in blood, in daylight to the ears,
saying: *My friend. Be calm.*
You are forgiven, even
unto death. The lion
places his soft paw
on the shoulder of a man:
This is my peaceable son;
my fond intention, dreaming,
even unto death. The sun blazes.

The animals lie down.
Everywhere the ground trembles
with their muscular sleep.
The man disappears, as though
he was not ever in that house at all,

but was invisible, or asleep
deep in the lion's dark belly,
or was the lion, dreaming of him.

THE YOUNG WIFE

1

Holding our hands to the light,
we saw wings beating
the blood in the wrists.
A man's hand relaxes
into a cup, a woman's
reaches toward the man's,
or what he was reaching for,
which is nearer her. Turned
off the lights, over
the bed, & everywhere.

2

Nights when it rains in the Midwest
it means different things: how steel rails
flash momentarily behind the last sleeping-car,
or to a farmer, listening in the night,
if this kind of solitude is worth it.

3

If I appeared to have fallen into doubt,
or to have taken myself seriously—
that's all right. I seemed to be dying there.
Not alone, really, but out of sight, which
is the same thing, only smaller.

4

I have a name sewn to my scarf—
that's like saying who I am.

Unspoken, it could be "Knowledge"
or "Bad Dream." Whenever
you speak to me, I am still
young enough to be surprised.
Which is like saying there are
promises I cannot keep.

ODALISQUE

Vacuuming naked
this morning, balancing
on her puffed, white stomach

the silver head of a dog
(a chained medallion),
she whispers desperately.

The cold coin rises
consciously taking her breath,
the morning,

right out of her lungs.
Eyes, red obsidian
and black,

leap at her face
& the jaw snaps back
against her left breast

and her heart.
Is she whispering: *Love me?*
The child

in her belly awakens, turns:
Countess, Lover,
here I am,

dangling from my watch chain.
Over the sly
wheeze of the machine

it sucks at her heart,
blindly, as if in love.
Both of them dream then, awake.

The dog's head
swings on its chain
forward & back,

a cold hand on her chest,
and pushing its legs
deep within her thighs,

the child walks.

AVIATORS

We learned, and slowly, only
that we fell in the high spiral

of confusion. The millionth run—
and now our lives unwound.

Well, we had always had bright flak at heart.
And when we stalled our bomber under

the new moon, and emerged—who could have known?
In that musical dangle, jukebox angels

fed us their sweet compassionate bread.
Our bellies grew round as the red moon,

and we starved. Who could survive
desire? They have wired

our wild hearts for sound. We are falling down
forever toward your blue receding town.

THE PRIVATE LINE

It's me again. Nights
I lie, hot,
under the electric light,

deep in my own soup.
The personal red radio
I am desiring

beats back: "Hello
Lover." Home again:
the anxious angel,

wings in my darkest bowel.
That's Jonathan's bed,
singing. I'm thinking

maybe it's the mad
who circle up the bedsprings;
or the dead

are really here, signaling.
For the sake of
no one, I'm still awake,

hearing the filaments sing.
And no one is here
under the angel's wing, his

irrelevant tongue in my ear.

SONG OF THE REFUGEE

I found, in my own room:
an open drawer, piety
on my key chain, thoughts
without hair. I
was an eye that looked away.

I put my head
on my bald
chest. (I was an egg!)

That was the end
of kidding myself.
                      But later
notes from former
friends were pinned to the walls,
locks of their longest hair,
greetings for every season.

Convalescence,
with my bags
locked in his wagon, looked in.
I was eating my second supper.
I said: Brother,
but for you
look what they'd have forgotten.

He couldn't be fooled.

He sold everything: rings,
silver, my Portable Rilke;
he gnawed holes
in my brightest clothes,
barked at the postman, and
moved in.

I wanted to be
the man who remembered everyone,
the biggest cathedral,

and here I am, the confessor.

THE MONUMENT TO
RESIGNATION

Then I was crazy,
wearing my solitude lightly—
the colored duck

breeding war in a thatched hut—
but I couldn't have loved you less.

I washed my weapons in
the day's events; went out,
armed, at night.

My door
opened on the new unknown.
I threw stones

at the houses of starlets,
then ran off, colorless,
into the shadows.

But the danger wouldn't disappear.
No one would let me in.
My house
was a column of salt.

So I left, living
for years on water and grain.

And one spring morning
I passed by and
laid this poem, like an ordinary head,
on my old doorstep.

LOOKING FOR JONATHAN

Before sunrise
the sky whitened. I said
to myself: "Whatever troubles you,
leave it."
        Then we're speeding
into the fields,
    corn, white houses,
buses at daybreak: the same eyes
we've brought along before.

  But the yellow light
looked
    in at us: "That discomfiture—
give it here."

O, I knew what
had been planned, but where?
    And in whose name?

Non-Fiction, happiest man, ran alongside,
    then right-angled "See you—"
into the white woods.
    We followed, of course, on foot.

There, various women (some I knew
    or had known) were dancing, filling
    a clearing.
                The pond:
We swam in the old way, lit
    the green leaves to grow warm.
Our smoke rose into the sun.

When I saw America, she had danced all night,
she was chalk-white
leaning on her husband's arm.

                    I could see
the orange home town, coming.
I leaned honestly
        into my own reflection.
I had no more stories of God.

THE HISTORY

OF PSYCHOTHERAPY

I find many dishes
lie on the dark lawn, waiting.

Now for the history of love:

A man found a locket
—or amulet—
anyway, a real disc, cold
silver in his bed.
He opened it.
Much of the rest

is an underground journey, soft noses
   of moles,
running water,
the occasional
distant emergencies: holding aliens
   or ships, in time of war.

In the end, he might arrive.
His childhoods
surprise him:
                 Thousands
of motionless, small toads.
But each sleeps, for love, in a dish.

The entire scene
is opening.
Clarity, I think I am
coming toward you, I bear
myself with such indifference.

PREPARATION FOR TRAVEL

Someone has lost a note from his mother.
Another has bad wings.
Also Reader I hope
you are home and between cool linens.

For although
the door opens, no one comes in.
       I am locked in a house
where everyone flies up.
  One by one God is removing us
  (pray for us).
His large head, like a horned
owl's, comes between the trees,

and I believe he is coming here.
  So that I hug my knees, learning
  solicitude:
         to watch my wristwatch, like
         a silkworm, spin.

The fortunate man sleeps—
  and his dream goes over the gates, gathering
speed, by dried ponds, lawns,
the constant headlights, and
   more peaceable homes.

When at last it rests,
       it is a sheet over the sea.
The angel also goes by,
coming here.
         And we, here,
outside the asylum's gate, are packing,
although there is no solution.

I hear the angel speak,
kindly,
but we are denied companions.

   For my birthday
God gave me 10,000 white birds, so that I
      would not be alone, but I am.
So I am writing to you,
the only poem I ever write; badly,
but in sincerity.
   I am trying to love you.
Love me. I have no shame.

for Linda

SPRING SONG

The raccoon lay down at dawn,
its little feet were pointing upward.
Even the tourists are sick.

And the daily, beneficial light
which had traveled a long time
toward us lies on its head
in meadows, and against trees.

It begins to surround us,
lighting the leaves easily,
some bark, the earth, a green stone.
We spread sheets over the ground.
Love is good. Who are you?
If I'm sullen, you'll mother it.

Just under the blue scum
of a pond, we, facing up, see
ourselves dramatically touch.
I'm sick of it all, I pull
your little breasts.
                    Oh it is
another morning; starving,
I've come around. Love,
muddy bitch, nothing is right;
it is the year of regrets,
why does the light come down?

ENTRANCE TO A MIRROR

This is a still life,
shade beneath which

configurations
come forward to you.

I am coming
toward you. The deep

chairs, the piano
and thin glass vases

darken behind me,
coming to the door.

Here is evening, here
are white roses and

my hand. The windows
stand very straight, as

if amazed, but are
closing now against

us and the light. Here
is your glass hand. In

our faces, roses
like whitened wax, shine.

DEATH'S ONLY SON

I wanted to be
brilliant glass, worn
at my throat.

Whoever I faced
would become clear to me.
I wanted to be Death's

only son, the favorite,
constantly refused.
Ritual, our bond.

I stand among friends,
representing them;
their flesh, like

damp bread, softens.
Now I am lonely.
And when they turn,

their mouths small
and old, I think
it is to speak of me.

Memory, we grow
restless, you & I,
and accidental.

DEATH & FRIENDS

(1970)

We are attempting to communicate,

but no communication between us can

abolish our fundamental difference.

If you die, it is not my death. . . .

GEORGES BATAILLE,
Death and Sensuality

I

THE PARACHUTIST

Then the air was perfect. And his descent
to the white earth slowed.
                                        Falling
became an ability to rest—as

the released breath
believes in life. Further down it snowed,

a confusion of slow novas
which his shoes touched upon, which seemed
as he fell by

to be rising. From every
small college and rural town:
    the clearest, iced blossoms of thought,

but gentle.
                        Then the housetops
of friends, who
he thought had been speaking of his arrival,
withdrew, each from another.

He saw that his friends
lived in a solitude they had not ever said aloud.

Strangely he thought this good.

    The world, in fact,
which in these moments he came toward,

seemed casual.
Had he been thinking this all along?

A life
where he belonged, having lived with himself

always, as a secret friend.

A few may have seen him then. In evidence:
the stopped dots
of children & dogs, sudden weave

    of a car—
acquaintances, circling up
into the adventure they imagined. They saw him drop

through the line breaks
and preciousness of art

down to the lake
which openly awaited him.
           Here the thin
  green ice allowed him in.

Some ran, and were late.
These would
forever imagine tragedy

(endless descent,
his face floating among the reeds,
unrecognized), as those

who imagine the silence of a guest
to be mysterious, or wrong.

THE TRUCKER

Elevators, like great oaks
rise into the evening, and when they descend
you hardly know yourself.
                    All night
the fair, shadowed cab light
shone on the trucker's face. If only
he had learned to think like that!

Some extremes, but much benign lack of interest,
for which the heart gradually opens.
. . . patiently working, bringing cattle

from Denver, sorghum, oats,
butter, wheat and pigs from the Midwest,
steel bars, the body

with its different nightly smells . . .
He wanted to walk the length of Kansas.
The years had not even been difficult,

but like the stars
he watched from the speeding cab,
spaced unevenly . . .
so many particular events.

PIERROT WITHOUT MEMORY

Leaves, like the shadows
of flying birds, turn at the window, now
this way, now that;
    unsure of where in this he belongs,

he sees himself
at a great distance in his dream:
running, now standing, just as he does daily,

but in the image's hands
are flowers, representing nostalgia,
        poor blues and grays. Then his dream

takes the shape of guarded biography, wherein
the dreamer
removes his hands from the world's face,

letting the arms drop, the uselessness,
rather than be wrong.

So he is transformed into the moon, a light
within stone
    which only may bear witness.
At last he is himself,

bearing his head, a great
liquid globe, into the streets. Of those of us

who are not awake,
he alone does not beg to be relieved.
    His part in this is only radiance.

Give me your love, poor blues and grays.

WHAT KEEPS US GRINNING

AT NIGHT

We thought sex was a root.
It would grow crooked, arthritic
& hard, very
relentless, serious, positive . . .

Those were the days!—
We could have inched into the earth;
we could have eaten for centuries
of the fat black;

we were gropers & long things.
Skinny & white,
we extended like tendrils
getting at the absolute.

Listen, as far back as you can remember
wasn't it quiet?
Wasn't it damp, you sluggard?
Wasn't the skull's wetness, whiteness

under your wife's face
what kept you grinning at night?

CREATIVE WRITING

The heart is a violent muscle; it opens & shuts.
The subject is death.
The subject is also laughter, the bravery
of girls, nine in a row.

In each face a hole opens.
Nine tiny stars of nervousness spin languidly out.

Sweethearts, death is blind,
he'll run up & down your bodies.
Death, with a dog's face
goes running through the Women's Dorm;
he has neither breasts nor jewelry.
Counselors run in his shadow, shouting Here,
We're all Christians here!

In the old country, everybody was Jewish.
Everybody had the smell of clothes soaked in a hot tub
and they learned to lament the fallen, the falling,
the about to be born.
Birth was painful, a long vibration
like the intake of breath after laughter.

I don't want to trouble you; you're entering history.
Your flesh is the moon's, gradual & broken.
Those boys are no consolation; they'll circle you,
    inscrutable calligraphy,
with no place to land.

I'm going to think about death until
my mouth runs. I'm going to look at death
with a face terrible as his own.

I don't want to scare you;
after death there are two alternatives,
both heartless:
memory & forgetfulness.

TO KILL A MAN

He who has not killed a man
Moves through the air in a daze.
     —Amharic warriors' song

Perhaps in snow.
Certainly by hand.
His, in your own,
grows slack.

Now it is permissible
to sit quietly.
His fingers tighten
in yours. Hours

watching the sun
move, the snow waver.
Then it's dark.
The field freezes.

Come out, rabbit,
this is safe—
And the mice, small
spots of nervousness.

But trust me,
there is nothing
left to lose
or witness.

The white owl
passes overhead.
The fox sleeps.
How can you know

his dream? I can.
Here is the hand.

THE EYE OF THE TRAVELER

1

Gray genitals of coffee
hang over the cup's lip. Even the egg
is bland in its spoon, a mild offense,
though warm. In the morning news
the wars go on. Before this meal
you want to believe that an affirmative
angel will lean down. For grace,
you say for grace.

2

Some men advance with aprons.
One drives in a truck, dropping sawdust
in a narrowing circle to be spread.
Now the animals enter; though they
are foolish and not to be told,
we believe they die in pain.
In January they slept standing,
a line of cold foreheads, facing north.
Now one will breathe like an opened faucet
down to the soft, hot floor. Whether
in dignity or confusion, he bows.
His snout cracks like a stone.

3

When you were driving to Tucson, your eye
went by itself, without destination,
for it was remarkably cast down.
That hitchhiker, who should
have been curious, or a gracious mirror

to shine back on you, slept
sitting up. Was he formidable?
You thought he carried the cold
iron of experience in his boot,
but he kept it there. His tongue clucked
lightly in his sleeping cheek.

4

Maybe the angel is experience. The animal
and the traveler might know him by belief.
We move into the next storm
and the slaughterhouse without regret.
It is morning; the animals fall down,
their bodies silently steam.
Coffee scalds the air above the cup.
Maybe like a miracle because it
is common, a man who walks upright
drinks his coffee and departs.
His head nods as he walks, a blind,
or holy, affirmative machine.

II

THE CAMPAIGN FOR PEACE
IN OUR TIME

Once in an adolescent sweat
we planned all night to be righteous;
to be never without poverty
and always unreasonably gentle
(how could they forgive us?)
like fathers, to our wives.

The campaign for peace in our time
distracts, like the coffee talk of saints.
Compassion is a kind of whip
I don't use well—but if I were ardent,
walking into the fields
or over the snow with a step less social,
then I could walk forever . . .

The saint flagellates himself; it seems
to be another man. Not pain,
but the aesthetic of pain is learned.
He knows there is no reward for being hurt.
Slowly he strips his skin.

What a beautiful mistake!
You, or I, the poor men—we who are
neither gentle nor killers in a bad cause—
did we find that vacant, flayed skin
and mistake it for a coat?
We are terrified, we are pleased
to wear it, into the streets
and at last to our journals and beds.

———

From that coat of pain
a certain voice which is half ours
speaks openly, and entertains our lives.
But the campaign for living with ourselves
which was a saint who became free
is moving swiftly now into the fields,
gliding over the snow—
a heart of great lightness, grown
altogether practical and strange.

THE SOLITUDE OF HIGH OFFICE

JOHN KENNEDY

Imagine it: a man whose fingers
grow like redwoods into the century,
a row of proclamations.
It is a partial change: into the lives
of men who are themselves
lives of their fathers, the stories
told to them as children.

I mean the stories of how kings wept,
in the arms of their children,
and the solitude of high office.
We saw the streets we had been walking,
not of gold, but stone.

By his death, of a value
not intentional, saying in the slow traffic—
and when there is silence
like a tree spread over the picnic
or standing in the child's room—
here again is the story of kings: now
how we must love ourselves.

THE NEXT PRESIDENT

From the cracked bodies of insects
for his protection
we will construct a shell of brown enamel,
which at the first blow will shatter.
We make ourselves ready by treachery.

For his fingers, eight keys,
which in continually changing combination
will allow him entrance, into his house & office.
These are named force, childhood, accuracy,
the cave, potty, Sebastian Bach,
the key & need. At his prayer
the crossing of thumbs will signify assassination.

The grave:
topped by carved angels, in the manner of New England,
each with a child's face.
Here in each pupil we have bleached the stone
where the bullet may enter.

But he will be the one we do not murder,
who has no place in our affections.
He leaves an alternative:
we may punish
ourselves without cause, & be free.

He will have so little need of us
as to rise daily from the dark Potomac
into our contemporariness, like mercury in bread,
the eight keys raised to bless,
the eyes blind, fixed within.

THE ROBOTS,

THE CITY OF PARADISE

Out of the knowledge you mysteriously left
came oil, steel, art,
ways to duplicate ourselves.

Year-of-Our-Makers-X, world without nations,
wherein we walk, fearless, under the dead lamps,
hardly bothering to care. Our shadows
cross your dark shop displays; our purposes
slowly forgettable, though faithful to your plan.

Your aluminum police, our angels, soar . . .
Everywhere the new pattern
is ourselves, believing in necessity, as you
in our memories did not.

City of Paradise: commitment to a powerful,
abandoning instruction. We stand
like citizens, like lambs without banners,
under the best of all lives,
liking it, yours.

THE SPOONS

We're eating your lies,
ashes in silver spoons;

impossible not to hate you!
No, not your lies—

your demands,
burned, your plans for our lives.

We should be done.
The spoons are still cracking,

are we beating our skulls?
Like children, like

convicts. Thank you,
at last we are doing everything wrong!

OF GOVERNMENT

Of necessity, the women lie down like maps.
The men are beautiful divisible numbers.
Tragic & insubstantial, *he* moves on *her* landscape,
a particular sequence we will call believable.

So now we are adult. Each of us
is a little mother, rediscovering seriousness:
how around a table the arrangement of dolls
frowned, without breasts, into their tea
one day and refused to speak.

In bed, we are as political as children.
It reaches *that* far, the idea of government,
controlled movement of traffic & arms.
Then we are masses of emotion
needing direction to be trusted?

The marriage directive is: Adjust.
The movement of men over women is friendly,
and, for a moment, light, then stalls.
Then slides away, like a land mass
into the sea.
                    The directive of government
is: Diplomacy. Like courtship,
it fears and displays the erotic;
like marriage, it cultivates the bored.

Boredom, the single indignity worth repetition.

Some indifferences take care of us,
but eventually each is an angry father:
the artist's scorn for his audience;

hatred of the child for the parent
who, by love, permits no escape.

Failing at love, we find it was not important.
Better to be honest than to be human,
though both are contained in a pure, relentless anger:
hatred of opposites, of sex, of directives,
hatred of ourselves, and boredom with that hate.

So we move toward heaven, man and wife
and nation, not hoping to find it,
but by some violences done to ourselves
(by marriage, by government) to reveal ourselves.

Lacking belief, we are the dolls we once kept.
One day they would not be arranged
but stared into *our* government (which was,
we then believed, of love), were undeceived,
and trusted, at last, the richness of the world.

IT'S THE BEGINNING;

SO MUCH FOR SENTIMENT

But when we trudged uphill, noting
the sooty mass of snow, watching the chimneys
grow dark with twilight; there we were,
and the way was tedious. Time to procrastinate.

Here is a heap of fat: it sucks
its cigar, makes plans; it even contemplates.
Your neurosis, an unbelievable pressure,
can stand in itself like a cow.

In the face of the loved friend
you see a door, his own loneliness;
beyond, the meadow and trees.
The secular root of the bad dream
was always ourselves, most difficult.

So there we were, and it *was* the beginning,
chewing our useless intentions.
Out of them came soft, metallic gowns.
It was a kind of progress: we slept,
dreamless, cold and protected.

Oh but daily we were all hot with lamentations!
Slowly they grew into the wrong mountain:
a strategy, destroy it!

Depend on the friend's face, his good intent,
his willingness to allow some deception.
An unbelievable pressure is lean and hungry.
Starve it, love it, put your head into it,

it is the new year, build into it
instruments of instruction which will terminate.
Is it the right beginning? We march into it;
it is open all around like a meadow;
we come naked, sweet as tea, secular, joyless, intent.

III

BELIEVER IN PAIN

Jerusalem
the city a word
the word is *illuminant*

or *oil* a lubricant
I desire to be magnanimous
it is desire

a man's joy
a woman's pain upon
which all the nations rise

in the dark
at the olive's center
we lie disturbed

in death the flesh oil & solid
in love squeezing it forth
in birth skidding out on it

wounds blackened
of the saints
oiled & bound in Jerusalem

oil of the wringing of hands
castile of the boiled animal
the greases of labor

Jerusalem hidden
in a field of petroleum
well hidden inside the sentry's whistle

in the graves
flesh waits for the rain
the sewers glisten

the soul
in its oiled boat
believer in pain come forth

A LETTER

I put my soul in a tin dish.
All night
the possum lapped.

Next I put

I put my brain in the tin dish,
it was slick.

I put my brain in the tin dish,
god-awful.

I put my brain in the tin dish,
the brain pan,
the bowl. I didn't want it.

One night
my hand became a tarantula.

But I kissed its head,
I put my mouth down in the dark fur, turned
it over, breathed

into the warm belly of palm.
And such repose, David,
came over me . . .

But the other one,
the hairless one,
was a hand. It shook in fear.

Now I have two hands, no
intellect, and each
refuses to cut off the hated other.

3

Every year I feel older; it's normal,
a task I don't love, & haven't
the time to hate.
Powerless, now

I walk out.
And, inarticulate, I breathe into the faces

of the undergraduates. A girl
said, "Mr. Anderson,
you *know* so much," & I touched her; but

my good hand
ran along my face: its wilderness.

4

And, David,
but for love of you (& some
others) I'd give up. You said,

"I can't find my life, either."
It falls all winter;
it falls into your hair & your eyes, making

them wet again:
the lost freshness
for which we hurt ourselves, and write these letters.

for David Schloss

LECTURE WITH SLIDES

The city, very white, extends
for a few miles; around it
is nothing important. Its streets
are not crowded, or dirty.
Partially submerged in entrances,
the women are indistinct; dress, often
the color of dust. Happiness is not
important. If you have been walking, it seems
endlessly, in those blazing streets
there is always a shop open.

A traveler from the Mediterranean spoke.
But it was just beyond remembering;
nor did he interest you.
The problem might be selfishness.
But if so, it is intentional, like
a man turning from love. Later you made
some remarks, meant to be polite,
which he took seriously.

And in the classical gray women
there was that lovelessness
you sought. You were approaching
a middle age. Had you
anything to say for yourself?

ROWING AT DAWN

The summer of 1940
has risen again, slowly, like the white
incandescent back of a swimmer.
Here are the unborn: one light
in a lightless pond
into which the first signal
will be courage, causing them pain.
Into their dream
the oar of the new world dips & pulls.
Slowly the rain
is light upon their shoulders, *Come,*
here is July, the month
of your birth, into which water runs.
All over Europe
sirens unwind into the morning.
The parents moan, like nations bearing sheep.

It is possible to believe in the day
without confusion, to find
the light coming between some trees,
unmemorized. It is possible to move
openly among one's discontents,
to love the enemy, to bear
witness with an honesty which is kind,
because direct. Sleeping
I believe this. But in a dream
the voices of the unborn clarify and rise:
    Come, it is still the beginning
    we will eat the dark
    muscle of our mothers' hearts
    and drift forever into evening . . .

DROWNING

Out of my hands. Awhile
without breath, letting go, some stories
in which I recognize myself—
that solemnity
which in a former life I kept from you,
that, here, is sleep.
So let me go.
Resigned, I am at last kept wholly
only by you.
Drifting above your bed,
here are my hands,
head, feet, the five white islands
turning & joined.
                    Only when you sleep
without memory,
my body is like bread, coming apart.
Released, the blood rests
or falls, drawn downward into your lungs—
your breath is small,
dark clouds which dissipate.
Slowly, almost without weight
the tubes & secret chambers
of my body fall toward you, covering,
then dissolve. What love
you had for me
rests, a cleared intelligence on your face.
Now it is nothing human: water,
or air,
or charity without belief.

WALKING BAREFOOT

In the morning,
I'm not used to it . . .
and the dew
burns; I had thought
to give up every kind of pain.

There is the other life
without passion or memory.
It goes alongside.

It is the turtle's shadow.
It is the snail's shadow.

In each of my steps the grass darkens,
filled with discontent.

THINKING OF DEATH

The sleep was in me.
He was thinking
of that night on the beach, the sleeping bag
a coat full of weariness.
Just below his head
the water, a dark animal
with no face,
advanced. He dreamed of combing his hair.

Some men marry, he said,
but I am thinking
of death, always. What a gentle wife.

In November, 1968,
I'm sick on pills and sleeplessness;
my gentle wife is no help
though she touches my hair.

Who can we pray to next, who has
a bag of salt
in which to carry us home?
I have never been so far from my own death,
so far from the personal.

WALKING IN THE OPEN

1

Walking in the open
with three friends, we came
slowly out of our conversation
up a small hill, then down, breathing,
to this place I now set before myself again:
a field, where I felt recognized.
There was no tree, but myself
at the center of three friends,
each of us vulnerable,
each of us silent and walking . . .

2

In the north I have come to imagine
the lakes are cold, filled
with clarity. And in their houses
I believe my friends, who
are alone, shower and sleep.
Rooms fill with their breathing,
which will die. The fields
we have walked toward
are diminished; yards break outward
past landfall and the last,
desperate intuition: if I saw
you there, I would refuse you . . .

3

But I want to be what you ask.
In that northern country
blood burns a trail; the snow

is hurt by it. I want to be hurt by it,
running with the small animal's terror
into the next thing, courage;
and, surviving, the necessity of care . . .

A PHOTOGRAPH OF MYSELF

Surely in my eyes that light is now lost,
or has deepened; and my hand, which
in the photograph seems tense
and strong, is less sure.
                                        Is it
the right hand? Yes, it is still
lean, and larger now;

enough to hold this small, boy's hand
within it, like a son's,

perhaps to reassure him, as I do not
my own sons, who are not yet born.
    Across the gray garden

stand some men; I do not know them.

Nor, I think, does he. But they stand firm,
    a terrible simplicity
which will disappear. So, too, the other,
unknown, as far from him

as my living self, who again
clicks the shutter.
    He did not know it would reach this far.

    But it's not real, the boy,
myself, looking out at me but not seeing,

and the garden, which never grows.
    Good friend, believe me,
here I am, perhaps your best intention;

———

my hand can hold now your entirely small body.
   I can love you;
you are the friend's son, myself,

to whom I speak and listen.

EACH DAY DOES THAT

It seems, before sleep, something has been dishonest;
I'd like it to have been the day.

It is the recognition of a circle, some mild agreement
made as a child to behave, by which I could assign
myself the center of all things: a passive nature.

I sometimes write from an "occupation"—mailman—car-
        diac—
those whose lives are honest because without perspective.
They begin to value their loneliness. They grow tragic
and beautifully antique.

If these could meet, say in a conspiracy designed to fail,
they might agree: "I never met a man I didn't like."
Of all confessions, the worst!

Had I arrived, I'd say: "Resignation, the acceptance of
the reasonably tragic, is why I made you." They would
tear up their former maxims and begin to compete.

Once I wanted my readers to cry; now it's my personae.
Things are getting hot.

But the truth is I'm getting older. Most of my definitions
turn out to have been early promises, now more and
more forgettable.

Just before sleep, when I'm afraid, a few of those poems
which I had thought to be distant turn their small,
interested faces.

Never plain enough, or true enough, but their intention
turns my body, which had been weak with stubbornness,
toward home.

My parents lie like children in the dark. I'm not close
enough to hear them speak. But their love for each other,
which once seemed small to me, is there, and I can sleep.

IN SEPIA

[1974]

The place we occupy seems all the world.

JOHN CLARE
"November"

I

JOHN CLARE

I know there is a worm in the human heart,
In its wake such emptiness as sleep should require.

Toward dawn, there was an undirected light the color of
    steel;
The aspens, thin, vaguely parallel strips of slate,
Blew across each other in that light.
                        I went out
Having all night suffered my confusion, &
Was quieted by this.
                But the earth
Vegetable rock or water that had been our salvation
Is mostly passed now, into the keeping of John Clare,
Alive,
       whose poetry simplified us—we owe the world
          ourselves—
Who, dead or sleeping, now reads the detail leaf & stone
Passing, until it will finally be memorized & done.

I know the heart can be hard, & from this
Misgiving about itself, will make a man merciless.
I know that John Clare's madness nature could not
    straighten.

If there is a worm in the heart, & chamber it has bitten
    out,
I will protect that emptiness until it is large enough.
In it will be a light the color of steel
& landscape, into which the traveler might set out.

ROSEBUD

There is a place in Montana where the grass stands up
     two feet,
Yellow grass, white grass, the wind
On it like locust wings & the same shine.
Facing what I think was south, I could see a broad valley
& river, miles into the valley, that looked black & then
     trees.
To the west was more prairie, darker
Than where we stood, because the clouds
Covered it; a long shadow, like the edge of rain, racing
     toward us.
We had been driving all day, & the day before through
     South Dakota
Along the Rosebud, where the Sioux
Are now farmers, & go to school, & look like everyone.
In the reservation town there was a Sioux museum
& "trading post," some implements inside: a longbow
Of shined wood that lay in its glass case, reflecting light.
The walls were covered with framed photographs,
The Oglala posed in fine dress in front of a few huts,
Some horses nearby: a feeling, even in those photographs
The size of a book, of spaciousness.
I wanted to ask about a Sioux holy man, whose life
I had recently read, & whose vision had gone on
     hopelessly
Past its time: I believed then that only a great loss
Could make us feel small enough to begin again.
The woman behind the counter
Talked endlessly on; there was no difference I could see
Between us, so I never asked.

                    The place in Montana
Was the *Greasy Grass* where Custer & the Seventh

134

Cavalry fell,
A last important victory for the tribes. We had been
    driving
All day, hypnotized, & when we got out to enter
The small, flat American tourist center we began to
    argue,
And later, walking between the dry grass & reading
    plaques,
My wife made an ironic comment: I believe it hurt the
    land, not
Intentionally; it was only meant to hold us apart.
Later I read of Benteen & Ross & those who escaped,
But what I felt then was final: lying down, face
Against the warm side of a horse, & feeling the lulls
    endlessly,
The silences just before death. The place might stand for
    death,
Every loss rejoined in a wide place;
Or it is rest, as it was after the long drive,
Nothing for miles but grass, a long valley to the south
& living in history. Or it is just a way of living
Gone, like our own, every moment.
Because what I have to do daily & what is done to me
Are a number of small indignities, I have to trust that
Many things we all say to each other are not intentional,
That every indirect word will accumulate
Over the earth, & now, when we may be approaching
Something final, it seems important not to hurt the land.

A COMMITMENT

After I watched your face, behind its mask
Of talk, deaden, then grow animate,
Alternating light & dark as you bowed
& drew yourself erect under the lamplight
Of someone else's room in which we talked,
I was restored. Though in the minor
Darkness of my heart, where I'm most alone,
I wanted to take your masculine face
Between my hands & press for strength.
The skull, for me, is death & strength,
Merely objective in a world of sense.

Within a month you lost your wife & friend.
But not to death. I knew their leaving
Had the appearance of a judgment on your life.
Because the friend was also mine & gone,
Because I loved your wife, in you or apart,
And because you wouldn't turn aside, I tilted
The lampshade down & drifted with you
On the edge of dark.

                              I remembered an evening
With friends in a small boat on a lake.
It was September: the late afternoon light
& wine we drank warmed us to each other.
Our quietness then passed from the shadows
Of trees close to the water—it seemed
We had drifted out over a great emptiness,
Silent, held only by our composure . . .

I think, now, of those friends: I
Let them go. Really, only for the ease
Of letting go. Now when I visit & attend

Their lives, they are partly strange; I know
My hesitations seem to judge their house.

I wanted to say, as I watched you steady
Yourself in the dark, I was restored
By your bearing & openness to pain,
A commitment to what you had already lost.
Our talk was personal; I said it in another way.

But if all our losses are a mirror
In which we see ourselves advance,
I believe in its terrible, empty reflection,
Its progress from judgment toward compassion.

for Steve Orlen

THE JOURNEY FROM ESSEX,

JULY 1841

At age 48, being of unsound mind,
Removed by his own volition from public life,
Escaped July 18, High Beech Epping Asylum,
Walking six days with little food, few words
Spoken only to strangers, to beg
Directions & some bread, arrived:
So here I am homeless at home & half
Gratified to be anywhere.
                              —John Clare

Removed again to Northampton (December)
Where he died,
Though for twenty-five years there
Was allowed some kindness,
Encouragement of his verse
& some small land on which to garden.

                    •

Kindly kept prisoner those hundred seasons,
Aware of the heart's affection for dark misguidance,
Failed of marriage & ambition,
Please John Clare, there was time
To put consequence aside & set out for home again.
Because your poetry simplifies us
We are the earth's innocence,
Alone, in no one's care . . .

                    John Clare,
So you may stay at home,
I will try to hold back some harshness.
Nor judge myself continually, or any man.

POEMS FROM THE CHINESE

How could I oversleep this spring morning?
The music of birds surrounds my awakening.

Then I remember last night's wind & rain,
How many blossoms have fallen while I slept.

·

Far from the city, I lean on an open porch.
An occasional tree bows with its summer weight.
The dogs run in circles snapping at flies,
Fish rise in the river to nibble at raindrops.

Ten thousand families in that far city
But here—only two or three small homes.

·

As I've grown older, I've taken to solitude.
I wonder what ambition brought me here.

I walk in the chill, forgetting to button my coat,
& sometimes by moonlight mutter to no one.

You ask me why my life is such confusion!

·

Even after it rains the hills are dry.
The moon catches in pine branches
& in the evening we feel a touch of autumn.

The stream is so clear now stones seem to float away.
Children going home rattle milkweed stalks.
The fisherman's boat nudges the reeds aside.

Did this spring, again, so casually slip away.

Please let's drink one last cup of wine—
When you leave this house, who will be your friend?

•

In the river mist I tied my boat to the bank.
I have a wanderer's sadness at evening.

Here, between earth & heaven, a tree can be lost,
But on the water the moon shines beside me.

•

A few stars,
Mostly silence.
At my window, the morning oriole,
                  the narrow moon.
Willows lean in the wind; a few leaves drift.

I find myself
Hesitant at my door:
Everywhere the year's regrets.
                  Cares seem to have no end.
Among them, like a dream . . . one remembered joy . . .

•

No one comes to this wilderness,
Only a sound like far-off conversation.

Shadows drift back among the trees.
Again the moss shines green with sunlight.

IN AUTUMN

At day's light
I dressed my cold body & went out.
Calling the dogs, I climbed the west hill,
Threw cut wood down to the road for hauling.
Done, there was a kind of exultation
That wanted to go on; I made my way
Up through briers & vines
To a great stone that rises at the hill's brow,
Large enough to stand on. The river
Below was a thick, dark line.
My house was quaint.
I sat, not thoughtful,
Lost in the body awhile,
Then came down the back way, winding
Through stands of cedar & pine.

I can tell you where I live.
My grief is that I bear no grief
& so I bear myself. I know I live apart.
But have had long evenings of conversation,
The faces of which betrayed
No separation from a place or time. Now,
In the middle of my life,
A woman of delicate bearing gives me
Her hand, & friends
Are so enclosed within my reasoning
I am occasionally them.

When I had finally stood, high above
The house, land, my life's slow dream,
For a moment I was required
To turn to those deep rows of cedar,
& would have gone

On walking endlessly in.
I understand by the body's knowledge
I will not begin again.
But it was October: leaves
In the yellowed light were altered & familiar.
We who have changed, & have
No hope of change, must now love
The passage of time.

II

A BRIDGE IN FOG

Cars at a great distance crossed in a line.
Below, the boats went forward towing their lights.
When I came to myself, I was divided within myself;
Merely for solace, I'd been watching a long time

& was still troubled as I turned toward home.
In its dark windows I could see myself approach,
So suffered my strangeness in reflection.
My wife was asleep. I was glad to be alone.

It was not for the scene I'd stood transfixed,
Only its lights' methodical passage by water,
& above, where the cars' beams flickered in mist . . .

Just before sleep I've traveled awhile like this.

THOUGH I LONG TO BE NO ONE

I passed for two nights
& days, alone,
On a train.

Whatever I do
I am always leaving.
Whoever's face I lay my own along,
The cheekbones bruised & rose.

Faces of friends,
Of women;
The elongated face of my third wife, aged
& concerned about my house . . .

Nightly I carry them forward in sleep,
Though I long to be no one.

The wheels of iron pass
Over these rails
& boards above water.
Over the bodies of my constant departure
Into my constant longing.

THE DAYS

All day I bear myself to such reward:
I close my eyes, I can't sleep,
The trees are whispering flat as water.

My friends' grayed faces
Do not alter with the weather anymore.
We sit by a cold stove & talk.
We suffer the terrible news.

Into a world made over & over
You rise each day,
You remember,
& something goes wrong.

God, if I had a wish, I swear
I wouldn't know what to spend it on.

OTHER LIVES

The guest sits in her flowered chair.
She is like a lion,
All muscular potential.

When she leaps, you will die of embarrassment.
You will die of the domestic.
But she never will.

Those other lives,
Hers, everyone's, yours,
Are reserved, even from themselves.

You only fear their essence—
Coming from such distances
It is inscrutable, austere.

And you? . . . unworthy of its coldest glance.

In the mirror, another stares back
Because the face is depthless glass,
Silvered at the brain's back to reflect.

You have given your guest your hand.
Out in the night, she rises like a ghoul
Into the moon's face, laughing.

No, she is just walking to her car,
As you are walking to sleep,
That alabaster sea whose tides the moon controls.

APRIL

Lord, yearly
I have not learned,
But meet that early spring
Emptied again of heart.
I have bargained my love
For love of what that first cold
April day foretold:
In your arms is the exquisite pain,
It is your forehead leans,
Not mine. And if I yearn . . .
That is not anything.
For I have sent my loves away
& taken to my loin
Your first cold green & naked day.

SPRING SNOW

So now it's spring again,
If I live in a spare season
I prefer it so.

Last night's April snow
Came on us unprepared,
I found myself out walking alone.

Alone, I'd watch the snow
Fall down on Massachusetts, where I lived.
I didn't have anything then.

I thought I'd have a son
By now, by someone,
Out of the grace I'd grow.

It was myself I grew:
Starlight, snowfall, cold & dark,
Whatever I want I can outwalk.

I didn't have anything then.
Spring snow, when I can live again,
I'll put myself aside.

So let it fall.

THE SECRET OF POETRY

When I was lonely, I thought of death.
When I thought of death I was lonely.

I suppose this error will continue.
I shall enter each gray morning

Delighted by frost, which is death,
& the trees that stand alone in mist.

When I met my wife I was lonely.
Our child in her body is lonely.

I suppose this error will go on & on.
Mornings I kiss my wife's cold lips,

Nights her body, dripping with mist.
This is the error that fascinates.

I suppose you are secretly lonely,
Thinking of death, thinking of love.

I'd like, please, to leave on your sill
Just one cold flower, whose beauty

Would leave you inconsolable all day.
The secret of poetry is cruelty.

III

THE INNER GATE

At a certain time of my life
That failure I had long before surmised,
Which was a destiny born
Of self-consciousness, assured itself.

I felt I had been walking aimlessly
Between shops & houses, along
Narrow cobbled sidewalks,
Turning corners as they occurred
In a Mediterranean city.

Passing its stained fountains,
Galleries,
Gates behind which were narrow yards
Full of flowers & washing,
I had lost track of memory.

Out of my longing
I had invented this particular city.

Within its heart
A house,
A room,
A diary of aesthetic change.

Though I had seldom mentioned within it
Those events or names by which
I was compelled to write,
I had secretly thought to accrue a life:

To imply
The passage of time.
Of myself, as citizen, from here to here.

•

I became coldly hysterical.
I attempted some small injuries. Scraping
My forearm across the rough stucco of a house front,
My blood speckled it a dull brown,
The color of old tintypes.

This regulated motion enraged me.
Even the pain grew melancholy
With its obsessive pulse.

I thought of picking a fight,
Or entering a shop to bring my fist
Crashing down on its display case:
I saw a hand rising
Through brooches & rings, to meet my hand
In the shadowy glass.

I realized I would remember
Only my conception, not the act.

The man who would beat me was already recognized.
•

Perhaps I was stunned; my mind
Which seemed now to have conceived even itself,
Would not function beyond
A certain repetition:

I saw myself, seated at a desk
In a small room, rise
From writing again & again.
My vision, with each rising of the figure,
Crossed by inches the plain wood floor,
The desk on which a journal
Lay open, toward a window.

The room,
Its furniture & bare white walls,
Lay otherwise in shadow.

I did not know if I was waking, or passing
Deeper into an obsessive dream;
I could see the light, sloped roofs of the city,
& below, a courtyard,
High walled & windowless but for my own.

.

Then I began walking.
I felt the eyes of others watching, as if,
Among these streets,
These pastel storefronts & shades of my making,
I was recognizably foreign.

As I turned corner after corner
My anxiety steadied
To a form of relaxed pursuit.

I found myself following a group of men;
Among them, one
Who in a former life,
Before the nets or mirrors had descended
Upon all motion of history,
I had seen as my future.

That is, in his comfortable,
Terrible submission to the traps of the familiar,
I had seen my own progression.

.

One by one these men dissolved into doorways.
The afternoon grew less hot.

In my singularity of following
I was relieved, & seemed carried
On a small boat down those blue, winding streets,
Often in the shadows of trees.

He turned at the heavy iron gate
Of an alley, touched
His remaining friends' shoulders,
& entered.

·

So I had made my way,
Which was after all by chance, & effortless.

As I passed from gate to inner gate
& into a high-walled yard,
My bitterness ripened. Standing in the flowers
Below his window,
I watched as he ate & read;
I watched the narrow passage of stars
& as his light went out.

If he had stepped outside
I might have strangled him,
Only to see his face fill with blood.

I desired a single, terrible event,
The passage from which would measure time.

·

On a stone bench, beneath a tree,
A man is smoking.
He sits in a patience of shadows
Above which the stars turn slowly.

Now the first wheels rumble
Over cobblestone. An awning
Is lowered.
Shopkeepers shade their faces from the sun.

And if, this morning
I should turn & touch your face
Or caress your throat lightly,
As if in love . . .

This is not love, but care.
Yours is the world
I dream in when I fail to dream.

·

These are the raptures of falling in space forever.

IV

And sometimes, in those solemn hours,

I felt my life already lived and over:

as in old journals, we come upon a story

that seems our own, and speaks, then passes.

RILKE
The Book of Hours

COUNTING THE DAYS

Just as we wake up, yawn, & lift a shade to explore
(Always imperfectly amazed at subtle change, but limited
By expectations & the window's frame from which we
      gaze;
A yard: of weeds & dogs & brown boughs, though
Sometimes even the boughs are altered by falling snow),

So he is counting the days, the years, back toward
A serious initial thought: that he was *here,*
Was *someone,* was counting the days toward when
He would (today) count back: an important déjà vu.

Accompany him, please. This journey into dissolution
As memories become events, become anticipations,
Then dissolve, will empty us of our complex doubts.
You will certainly love yourselves as history: potential
Which only took a certain lovely, arbitrary route . . .

As on a December afternoon, the stillness of which
Engenders that image of falling snow, we now
Begin again that art our lives become.

REFUSALS

Sometimes we get down to loneliness
& poetry is just talking about things.
In the wake of those graceful verses,
Those boats loaded with spiced meat & jewels,
Is a silence meant to kill.

                                So you talk
About death; you expel it,
The sweets of dioxide, into the air.
And driving all night, in silence,
You see it flying by.
Is it sweet, that you love it so? You're not
A poor bastard yet; you give some affection . . .
Like alms, or smooth as cheese.

And you still love the loneliness in marriage:
Refusals of sex & shared meals, frustrated
Appetites, for which you slam a door.
For sex should retain its adolescent shyness,
Shouldn't it?
                          Or better to meet at sea,
Two dark gunboats that thump & shoot fire
All night, trying hard not to win.

These refusals begin to look like courage.
You're trying hard not to give in.

But you can't come down from yourself;
You wouldn't if you could.
So you end up speechless, writing it down:
That tapping all night is yourself.
   Mornings you wake up listless;
How could you choose this life, & how

Among friends, deny kindness? You keep your eye
At death—or death's abyss;
You never choose to drop.

Sometimes you refuse to put up with yourself
But you go on talking,
Thinking, maneuvering
Over the dark & chartless waters
& under mysterious orders not to come in.

EXILE

. . . the exile that belongs to oneself,
the interior exile.
—*Richard Howard*

We must have some statement from it, for now
We are keeping smaller ones, circumspect,

As when a man in the midst of self-argument
Turns bitterly aside. The countenance

Lost in itself will languish awhile,
As if memory were a buoyancy stunned,

Then sink. He begins a descent, as into
Experience—his inner space, or solitude.

Nothing so private as this resting place.
From it the heart rises, a red

Wet planet contracting in space
As if in pain or opposition to itself.

Meanwhile we, in a weak external light,
Infer second thought; or if unsure,

We assume his sudden distancing
Complementary to our own. Thus friendship

Like the moon releases its pull
& we slide back into our own lives.

Wrongly inspired by the indifference we assume,
Is it possible our lives, sustained

At last only by deep concentration
& by the conversations we fear might be running down,

Can be understood? Formerly we noticed experience.
It did not accurately repeat,

But our latest responses are now generalized.
Eventually we choose exile

& self-descent. If that inner universe,
Objective & in distant accord, affords some patience

Sometimes we see a man emerge, wholly himself.
Or ourselves choose love, a kind

Of concealment
So private we can hardly speak.

LEVEL

You were of a certain age where the days are-
        interchangeable.
Where formerly you had suffered introspection, &
        emerged,
& where formerly you had married, living a popular
        novel,
Now you were calm, though unsure, believing this calm
To be inconsolable, a long plain of ennui or private joy.

You had turned back momentarily then, though
To your surprise from concern rather than shock,
To settle a few things & acquaint yourself one last time.
Then as you embarked, as onto a flat field of water
Stepping lightly off, you remembered a foreshadowing:
An image of adults talking quietly in the backyard
& smoking, the evening a pale haze around their bodies.

Now that image in its familiarity takes care of you.
Another surprise: courage is not a requirement,
Because this new expansiveness, seeming always
To be a living extension of itself, only requires
Your presence; the slight pressure of your body.

But it is not all reassuring, this comfort,
For you belong to it. The world, & your small love for
        it,
Floats like the talk of the adults, & is barely mutable:
Now you will feel a nostalgia for it;
No longer will you consciously alter its events.

And friendship, & companionship, faces of young
        students
Which after the immediate pleasures of consent

Had settled into composure, always refreshing your life,
Must change value now; will be less quick & lovelier.
After a long time & if you again become articulate
Or can listen generously, it can be given to you
To be provident, though this is at the mercy of time
Among other dependencies, & is not assured.

THE EDGE

You rise each day, you make
Your little rounds, you sleep.

You rise to the edge of grief.
You fall at the edge of sleep.

A woman lies down, she smiles
Above her troubles, she sleeps.

You rise to the edge of appetite.
You fall at the edge of sleep.

A man lies down, his hand
Shadows his face, he sleeps.

You rise to the edge of his wound.
You fall at the edge of sleep.

You lie awake, you watch
The stars revolve, repeat.

You rise to the edge of the world.
You sleep, & then you sleep.

IN SEPIA

Often you walked at night, house lights made
    Nets of their lawns, your shadow
Briefly over them. You had been talking about
    Death, over & over. Often
You felt dishonest, though certainly some figure
    Moved in the dark yards, a parallel
Circumstance, keeping pace. By Death, you meant
    A change of character: He is
A step ahead, interlocutor, by whose whisper
    The future parts like water,

Allowing entrance. That was a way of facing it
    & circumventing it: Death
Was the person into whom you stepped. Life, then,
    Was a series of static events;
As: here the child, in sepia, climbs the front steps
    Dressed for winter. Even the snow
Is brown, &, no, he will never enter that house
    Because each passage, as into
A new life, requires his forgetfulness. Often you
    Would explore these photographs,

These memories, in sepia, of another life.
    Their use was tragic,
Evoking a circumstance, the particular fragments
    Of an always shattered past.
Death was process then, a release of nostalgia
    Leaving you free to change.
Perhaps you were wrong; but walking at night
    Each house got personal. Each
Had a father. He was reading a story so hopeless,
    So starless, we all belonged.

———

STORIES

. . . as in old journals, we come upon a story that
seems our own, and speaks, then passes.

This is a story declining, as landscape
    Into its elements.
You saw that, driving through the Midwest:

How at twilight certain trees, houses
    You pass, float
On a flat expansiveness—such plain

Seclusive bodies as the stages of memory
    That darken & go by.
Finally not much will have happened:

Some processions you can remember awhile
    Between which the land
Goes on, gliding without force toward
    Night & sleep.

                  •

You were telling a story. The story
    You lived was not
The same, though both had a loveliness

Which was years. And in the middle years
    You lost your way.
All winter the rain fell evenly down

& spring was mild. Evenings you took
    Your time, walking,
Coming home. What couples you passed

Talked quietly; bodies incomplete by dark,
      Hands touching, they
Glided by. The stars turned slowly
      Their exclusive joy.

                    .

From your neighbor the night divides you,
      & from yourself.
There was a dark, exclusive joy: the past.

All you had earned was passage. Fixed
      Points, by which
You measured time, a gradual lassitude

Had overcome. You accustomed yourself
      To the night. By
Lamplight, or firelight, you read

Yourself to sleep. These were your dreams:
      The steady motions
Of ships or seasons, by which disquietude
      You woke & read.

                    .

You had forgotten the words you wanted to say.
      I think you lay
Too often on a woman's breast. Now you were

Like those women who gathered on the shore
      Watching the ships;
Those heroes, their husbands, rose distantly

& dissolved. All of your constancy, now,
      Was only longing.
Most of it speechless, though often you wrote

Long letters, specific & even-toned, filled
	With ambiguous yearnings
For the absolute. You wrote about your work,
	Your wife, your home.

					.

How can I say this, only beginning to see
	Such understanding as
Can make you whole. These stories end, as

Always, in our gradual belief. They are
	The lands we live in,
The women we finally meet as friends,

The friends we overcome. We overcome
	Ourselves. The words
You wanted are that story we tell

Ourselves so often it is eventually real
	Or plain; so, much
The same measure, or passing of time,
	Where we dissolve.

YEARS

Sometimes in weariness I stop.
Because I've been lucky
I think the future must be plain.
Over the trees the stars are quite small.

My friends talk quietly
& we have all come to the same things.
Now if I die, I will
Inherit awhile their similar bodies.

Now if I listen
Someone is telling a story.
The characters met.
They enchanted each other by speech.

Though the stories they lived
Were not the same,
Many were distracted into love,
Slept, & woke alone, awhile serene.

NOTES

American Landscape with Clouds & a Zoo:

Passages appearing in quotations in "Lives of the Saints," I & II, are from the journals, letters & works of the poem's subjects.

"The Face of Dürer" is a Christlike self-portrait, full-face, from the year 1500; the italicized passage is inscribed on the painting.

In "Winter Light," the reference is to Clyde Sukeforth, the Dodgers' scout who signed Jackie Robinson, major league baseball's first black player. Knowledge of the trivia once saved me from an Early & Bad End at the hands of authority in 6th grade.

My grandfather ("Sunlight / 1944") over-painted hundreds of black & white contact photographs, particularly of sunsets, with watercolors. He died before I could retain any exact memories of him.

Looking for Jonathan:

The poems from *Looking for Jonathan* have been rearranged into the chronological order in which they were written.

In Sepia:

The quotation in "The Journey from Essex" is from John Clare's journal of his escape from High Beech Asylum. In fact, unguarded & allowed to wander at will in the woods bordering the asylum, Clare simply decided to go home.

In "Poems from the Chinese," while no substantial changes have been made in the imagery of each, many lines have been omitted or rearranged, sometimes entirely altering the emotive intention of the original. This was done to personalize the poems, meant to be read as a sequence. The poets are, in order: Meng Hao-jan, Tu Fu, three by Wang Wei, Meng Hao-jan again, Wen T'ing-yun, & Wang Wei again.

The first line of the third section of "Stories" is from Rilke's poem "People by Night."

A Note About the Author

*Jon Anderson was born in Lexington, Massachusetts in 1940
and raised there. After graduating the Writers' Workshop at
the University of Iowa, he taught in the English Department
at the University of Portland and the University of
Pittsburgh. He now lives in Tucson, Arizona, where he
teaches in the Creative Writing Program at
the University of Arizona.*